The 24/7 solution

Understanding leadership, time, business aspect of Home care and how to scale through

By

Hanh F. Bee

Copyright

Copyright Notice: © [2024] Hanh F. Bee All rights reserved. This book is protected by copyright laws, and you can't copy or share any part of it without getting a green light from me, except for small quotes used in reviews or non-profit educational stuff. If you need to use something more than that, hit me up at [HanhFBee.com] for permission.

Disclaimer

Just a heads-up, folks! What you're reading is meant to help you learn some new things, but it's not the be-all and end-all. I'm not your lawyer, doctor, or secret guru. I've done my best to make sure all the info is on point, but hey, nobody's perfect. If there's a goof or something's missing, I can't be on the hook for any trouble it might cause you. Before you go making big moves based on what you read here, talk to someone with the right credentials. And remember, if things go sideways, I can't be held responsible for any mishaps or misunderstandings. By diving into this book, you're promising not to drag me or my team into any mess that comes from using this info. You've got to handle any bumps on your own. Thanks for reading and stay savvy

Table of content

Copyright	**4**
Table of content	**6**
Introduction	**9**
My Journey from Difficulties to Advancement	9
The Defining moment	10
Overview of The Daily, Everyday Schedule	12
Chapter 1	**17**
Recovering Your Time	17
Recognizing Time Killers	18
Chapter 2	**25**
Establishing a Coordinated Management Group	25
Creating Shared Objectives	26
Chapter 3	**33**
Formulating Crucial KPIs	33
Knowing KPIs	34
Chapter 4	**45**
Enhancing Group Organization	45
Evaluating Your Present Group	46
Chapter 5	**57**
Putting Systems and Procedures in Place	57
SOPs, or standard operating procedures	58
Chapter 6	**70**
Growing Your Company	70

Taking Up New Sites	71
Chapter 7	**83**
Juggling Personal and Professional Life	83
Defining Limits	84
Chapter 8	**95**
Case Studies and Success Stories	95
Real-World Instances	95
Conclusion	**109**
Managing a Company That Doesn't Manage You	109
Summary of Important Techniques	110
Final Words	119

Introduction

My Journey from Difficulties to Advancement

I stayed on the verge of giving up my fantasy in 2011. My entire existence was being consumed by my home consideration company, which I had devoted my all to. What had begun as a noble endeavor to provide exceptional care to individuals in need had transformed into an overwhelming mammoth that left me exhausted, overwhelmed, and questioning my ability to continue. My life was being sacrificed in order to fulfill the constant demands of a nonstop activity. Yet, rather than stopping, I decided to leave on a groundbreaking excursion that would ultimately lead me to recover my time, scale my business, and accomplish an equilibrium that once appeared to be unthinkable.

This book, "The every minute of every day Arrangement is the finale of that expedition. It's an aide intended for house consideration business pioneers who finish up in a comparable scenario — pushed by an eagerness for care, however battling under the weight of functional tasks. I need to impart to you the processes, frameworks, and pieces of information that rescued my firm as well as caused it to develop past my core assumptions.

The Defining moment

The defining moment came at an extremely tough period when I was confronted with personal shortcomings, client concerns, and regulatory upheaval. I sat in my office late one evening, covered beneath a mountain of desk work, and felt absolutely crushed. It was at that period of despair that I recognized things needed to change. The business was running me, rather than the converse way around.

I started to hunt out arrangements. I read a lot, went to studios, and met with professionals on the subject. I eventually started to figure out a different strategy for handling my home consideration company. This strategy is predicated on getting my time back, building a solid managing team, establishing core key performance indicators (KPIs), and refining group structures to reduce regulatory expenses.

These advancements have utterly remarkable consequences. My company had grown from a single, struggling location to a thriving network of seven locations, providing 1,000,000 hours of care annually overall. Thanks to the frameworks I established, I was able to address this development without compromising the quality of care or my personal well-being.

This accomplishment required smart and challenging labor. I learned how to set realistic appointments, provide attainable goals, and use frameworks that streamlined work and increased output. Specifically, I discovered how to realign my group around a shared vision and standard goals, ensuring that everyone was working toward the same goals even when I wasn't around.

Overview of The Daily, Everyday Schedule

The purpose of "All day, every day Arrangement" is to guide you through a comparable amazing journey. Each part is brimming with practical advice, working systems, and real-world examples that you can immediately implement into your company. Here's a little preview of what to expect:

Recovering Your Time: To save time, identify time wasters, manage your schedule effectively, and allocate tasks to others.

Creating a Brought Together Managerial Group: Identify common goals, improve communication, and ensure that initiatives move forward even in your absence.

Establishing Foundational KPIs: Understand important metrics, use them to maximize revenue and benefit, and utilize data to make well-informed decisions.

Simplifying Group Design: Assess your current team, clearly define roles and responsibilities, and reduce legal costs without sacrificing quality.

Implementing Frameworks and Cycles: Specify standard operating procedures (SOPs), make use of automation tools, and make continuous improvements to your cycles.

Growing Your Company: Decisively expand into new regions, actively supervise progress, and maintain the high standards of care.

Adapting Personal and Professional Lives: Establish checkpoints, concentrate on self-care, and make long-term supportability plans.

You will get contextual assessments and progress tales from other pioneers in the home consideration sector who have used similar strategies with remarkable success throughout the whole book. Their experiences provide valuable insights and inspiration, letting you realize that you are not alone in your struggles and that solutions are attainable.

Keeping Up a Business That Doesn't Take You Over

Helping you manage a home consideration company that doesn't run you is one of this book's key goals. It has to do with getting back your time, striking a balance between work and life, and creating a company that can run smoothly without constant supervision from you. By putting the techniques described in these pages into practice, you will truly want to focus on what you do best — providing exceptional client care — while also enjoying the personal and professional fulfillment that you deserve.

Remind yourself that change is an interaction as you go out on this adventure. There will be challenges along the way, and it won't happen by accident. But you can transform a home consideration business into a thriving, sustainable endeavor that provides you both achievement and fulfillment if you have the correct approaches, creativity, and dedication.

I want you to join me on this journey, learn from my experiences, and discover the minute-by-minute schedule that may upend your home consideration company. We can do amazing things together, and I look forward to celebrating your victories along the way.

Chapter 1

Recovering Your Time

Maintaining a home consideration business is a requesting try that requires consistent consideration and commitment. For the vast majority of business pioneers, the tireless requests can rapidly prompt burnout and shortcoming. This part is devoted to assisting you with recovering your time by distinguishing time killers, executing powerful time usage techniques, and excelling at designation.

Recognizing Time Killers

The most important phase in recovering your time is to recognize the exercises and undertakings that are consuming additional time than they ought to. Time killers can be tricky, frequently taking on the appearance of important undertakings or inescapable interferences. Here are some normal time killers to keep an eye out for:

Superfluous Gatherings: Gatherings can be a critical channel on your time, particularly in the event that they miss the mark on clear plan or reason. Survey the needs of each gathering and consider options, for example, email updates or brief check-ins.

Wasteful Cycles: Obsolete or excess cycles can dial back activities. Consistently survey your work processes to distinguish and dispose of bottlenecks.

Consistent Interferences: Continuous interferences, whether from staff, clients, or calls, can disturb your concentration and efficiency. Lay out limits and set explicit times for tending to non urgent matters.

Performing multiple tasks: While it could appear to be effective, performing multiple tasks frequently prompts botches and diminished efficiency. Center around each errand in turn to further develop productivity and nature of work.

By perceiving these time killers, you can start to do whatever it may take to dispense with or relieve their effect on your timetable.

Techniques for Using time effectively

Whenever you have recognized the essential time killers in your everyday daily practice, the following stage is to carry out powerful time usage systems. These techniques will assist you with focusing on errands, deal with your responsibility, and make a more organized and useful workplace.

Focus on Assignments: Utilize the Eisenhower Lattice to arrange errands into four quadrants: dire and significant, significant yet not pressing, critical yet not significant, and neither earnest nor significant. Center around undertakings that are both critical and significant, and designate or concede those that are not.

Put forth Clear Objectives: Lay out clear, reachable objectives for you as well as your group. Separate bigger activities into more modest, sensible undertakings and set cutoff times to keep everybody on target.

Time Hindering: Allot explicit blocks of time for various exercises over the course of your day. This method assists you with keeping up with the center and guarantees that you devote time to your most significant assignments.

Use Innovation: Influence apparatuses and applications intended for using time effectively and efficiently. Schedule applications, task the board programming, and computerization devices can smooth out your work process and save significant time.

Survey and Reflect: Toward the finish of every day, require a couple of moments to audit what you achieved and plan for the following day. This reflection assists you with remaining coordinated and guarantees that nothing gets lost in the noise.

Carrying out these time usage systems can fundamentally improve your efficiency and permit you to take full advantage of your business day.

Assigning Really

Designation is a basic expertise for any business chief, yet it is frequently underutilized or clumsy. Successful designation includes allocating assignments to the ideal individuals and engaging them to take responsibility for obligations. Here are a few ways to designate really:

Recognize Delegable Errands: Figure out which undertakings can be assigned without compromising quality or results. Routine managerial errands, information passage, and certain client interchanges are in many cases great contenders for designation.

Pick the Perfect Individual: Match errands to colleagues in view of their abilities, experience, and current responsibility. Guarantee that the individual you agent to has the fundamental assets and backing to effectively follow through with the responsibility.

Give Clear Directions: While designating an errand, be explicit about what should be finished, the normal results, and the cutoff time.

Clear guidelines decrease errors and guarantee that the undertaking is finished to your norms.

Enable Your Group: Trust your colleagues to execute their obligations and stay away from continuously fussing over. Engaging your group fabricates certainty and cultivates a feeling of responsibility and responsibility.

Follow Up and Give Criticism: Consistently monitor the advancement of appointed undertakings and give valuable input. This keeps up with responsibility and takes into account any fundamental acclimations to be made speedily.

By becoming amazing at designation, you can save your chance to zero in on high priority errands and vital preparation, at last upgrading your business' effectiveness and efficiency.

Recovering your time is fundamental for keeping a solid work life balance and guaranteeing the outcome of your home consideration business. By distinguishing time killers, carrying out viable time usage systems, and designating errands fittingly, you can make a more proficient and useful workplace.

The procedures illustrated in this part are down to earth as well as fundamental for any business chief trying to flourish in the requesting field of home consideration. Embrace these systems, and you will set aside yourself with greater opportunity to zero in on the main thing — giving remarkable consideration to your clients and accomplishing your business objectives.

Chapter 2

Establishing a Coordinated Management Group

A cohesive administrative staff is essential to the success of any home care company. When everyone on your team collaborates well to achieve shared objectives, the whole thing runs more smoothly and is more robust. This chapter will walk you through creating effective communication techniques, defining shared objectives, and making sure that excellent leadership continues even when you are not there.

Creating Shared Objectives

Establishing shared goals is essential to coordinating the work of your administrative staff with your company's overarching vision and goals. Well-defined and mutually agreed upon objectives offer guidance, promote cooperation, and augment drive. Here's how to help your team develop goals that will work:

Establish the Vision and Mission: To begin, precisely state the goals and objectives of your company. This guarantees that everyone in the team is aware of the bigger picture of their work and lays the groundwork for goal-setting.

Involve the Team: Take part in goal-setting with your team. To make sure that the objectives take into account the team's combined knowledge and experience, promote cooperation and contribution. Participation like this encourages dedication and ownership.

SMART Objectives: Establish objectives that are Time Bound, Relevant, Specific, Measurable, and Achievable by using the SMART criteria. This framework aids in making sure that objectives are measurable, attainable, and in line with the aims of your company.

Align Objectives with Roles: Make sure that the objectives of every team member correspond with their individual roles and duties. Each employee may better understand how their efforts impact the company's success as a whole thanks to this alignment.

Review and Adjust as Needed: Review goals on a regular basis and make any adjustments. Your team will be able to adapt to shifting conditions and continue working toward their goals thanks to this flexibility.

Establishing shared objectives gives your team a unified direction, ensuring that everyone is pursuing the same aims and making a positive impact on the company's performance.

Techniques of Communication

A cohesive team is built on effective communication. It guarantees that everyone is knowledgeable, involved, and capable of productive teamwork. Productivity and morale within your team may be greatly increased by putting effective communication tactics into practice. Here's how to do it:

Regular Meetings: Arrange regular meetings to go over concerns, plan next steps, and talk about progress. To guarantee that they are focused and productive, these meetings have to have a well-defined agenda and goal.

Open Lines of Communication: Create an atmosphere where team members are at ease discussing ideas, worries, and criticism. To encourage continuous discussion, use a variety of communication methods, including email, instant messaging, and collaborative platforms.

Messaging that is Clear and Consistent: Make sure that all of your correspondence is precise, succinct, and consistent. As a result, there are fewer misunderstandings and everyone is in agreement.

Establish feedback loops in order to promote ongoing development. Ask your staff for input on a regular basis, and give them constructive criticism in return. This two-way dialogue promotes a culture of learning and growth and increases engagement.

Transparency: Be open and honest about choices, adjustments, and difficulties in business. Keeping your staff up to date fosters trust and aids in their comprehension of the context of their job.

You may establish a setting where communication is easy, teamwork is improved, and people feel informed and appreciated by putting these communication tactics into practice.

In charge when you're not there

Even when you're not there, the stability and growth of your company depend on having strong leadership. It takes thoughtful delegating and preparation to make sure your team can continue to work efficiently without you. Here's how to make this happen:

Empower Your Team: Provide your team members more authority and accountability by assigning them tasks. Give them the freedom to decide within their purview while fostering their own development.

Develop Leaders: Find team members who have the potential to be leaders and make an investment in their advancement. Provide them opportunity to assume leadership responsibilities, as well as training and guidance. This improves team performance overall and gets them ready to jump in when necessary.

Process Documentation: Make sure that every important process and procedure has a clear, readily available document. In your absence, this documentation serves as a resource for team members and contributes to maintaining consistency and quality.

Clearly defined Succession Plan: Create a succession plan that specifies who will assume particular duties in your absence. Share this strategy with your team so that everyone is aware of the expectations.

Frequent Check-Ins: Make sure to keep in regular contact with your team, even when you're away. Stay engaged and up to date on events and changes by using technology.

You can make sure that your company runs efficiently even when you're not there to supervise every last detail by empowering your staff and cultivating strong leaders.

Creating a cohesive administrative staff is crucial to your home care business's long-term success. You can build a resilient and cohesive team that is capable of great things by establishing shared objectives, putting good communication techniques into practice, and making sure that strong leadership is maintained in your absence. These tactics foster a cooperative and upbeat work atmosphere in addition to increasing your team's effectiveness and production. Accept these ideas, and as your staff collaborates to achieve common goals, you'll witness the growth of your company.

Chapter 3

Formulating Crucial KPIs

Key Performance Indicators (KPIs) are crucial instruments for gauging how well your company is running and accomplishing your strategic objectives. KPIs assist you in driving revenue and profit, identifying areas for development, and monitoring performance in the context of a home care firm. This chapter will provide you a thorough overview of KPIs, explain important measures that are especially pertinent to home care companies, and provide tips on how to use KPIs to improve the financial health of your company.

Knowing KPIs

Key Performance Indicators (KPIs) are measurable metrics that represent an organization's vital success components. They give an accurate picture of performance in relation to particular targets and goals. KPIs are essential for home care companies to track everything from financial success to customer happiness. This is a more thorough explanation of KPIs:

Definition and Goals: Key Performance Indicators (KPIs) are measurements that show how effectively your company is accomplishing its main goals. They are intended to assist you in making defensible judgments by providing you with useful insights into your operations.

KPIs may be divided into a number of different categories, including financial, operational, customer, and employee KPIs. Every kind offers perceptions into various facets of your business. For instance, revenue growth and profitability are examples of financial KPIs, whereas efficiency and care quality are examples of operational KPIs.

Good KPIs should have the following characteristics: they should be SMART (Specific, Measurable, Achievable, Relevant, and Timebound). This guarantees that they are measurable, understandable, and consistent with your company's goals.

Establishing KPIs entails figuring out which important aspects of your company are crucial to its success, selecting the right metrics to gauge these aspects, and establishing goals based on previous performance or industry standards.

Knowing what KPIs are and how they work can help you start identifying the precise measurements that will yield the most insightful data for your home care company.

Important KPIs for Home Care Companies

Home care companies work in a special setting where client happiness, care quality, and operational effectiveness are critical. Thus, it's critical to use KPIs that accurately represent these goals. The following crucial indicators are especially pertinent to home care companies:

1. Customer Contentment and Sustaining:

Client Satisfaction Score: Calculate your clients' level of satisfaction with the services you've rendered. Feedback forms and questionnaires can be used for this. High customer satisfaction ratings show that your customers are content and probably will stick with you.

Client Retention Rate: Monitor the proportion of customers who stick with you for an extended length of time. A high retention rate is indicative of a devoted customer base and reliable service.

2. Care Quality:

Care Plan Adherence: Keep an eye on how well your carers adhere to your care plans. This guarantees that patients receive the recommended degree of treatment and contributes to upholding high standards.

Reporting Incidents: Keep track of the quantity and kinds of reported occurrences (falls, medication mistakes, etc.). A low incidence rate indicates that safety procedures and care are working well.

3. Effectiveness of Operations:

Visit Compliance Rate: Calculate the proportion of planned visits that are carried out according to schedule. High compliance is a sign of dependability and efficient planning.

Average Visit Duration: Keep track of how long each visit typically lasts. This aids in determining the productivity of caregivers and guarantees that customers receive enough care.

4. Financial Results: Income per Customer: Determine the average amount of money made from each client. This aids in planning for expansion and evaluating the monetary contribution of certain clients.

Profit Margin: Monitor the variation between your earnings and outlays. A strong profit margin is a sign of sound money management.

5. Worker Contentment and Performance:

Rate of Employee Turnover: Calculate the pace at which workers depart from your company. Excessive turnover may be a sign of discontent and have an impact on the continuity of service.

Keep tabs on the proportion of caregivers who finish the necessary training courses. This guarantees that your staff has everything it needs to deliver top-notch care.

These indicators offer a thorough picture of the functioning of your home care company, taking into account staff performance, customer satisfaction, care quality, operational effectiveness, and financial stability.

Increasing Revenue and Profit using KPIs

KPIs are instruments for fostering progress and attaining corporate expansion; they are not only for measuring. Strategic use of KPIs may increase sales and profitability for your company. Here's how to do it:

1. Matching Business Objectives with KPIs:

Alignment on a strategic level: Make sure your KPIs are in line with your overarching company objectives. For example, concentrate on KPIs associated with customer acquisition and retention if your objective is to get a larger market share.

Establishing Objectives: Based on your strategic objectives, assign each KPI a clear, attainable aim. These goals will direct the work of your team and serve as a standard for achievement.

2. Observation and Evaluation:

Frequent Monitoring: To measure performance and spot patterns, keep an eye on your KPIs at all times. Your team may view and utilize data visualization by using dashboards and reports.

Root Cause Analysis: To identify the underlying problems when performance is below expectations, carry out a root cause analysis. This aids in the creation of focused improvement plans.

3. Making Decisions Based on Data:

Making Well-Informed Decisions Make well-informed judgments on your operations by utilizing KPI data. To find areas for improvement, for instance, examine feedback if your client retention rate is poor.

Resource Distribution: Distribute resources according to KPI achievement. Increase your investment in sectors that have room to develop and improve underperforming regions.

4. Ongoing Enhancement: Benchmarking: To assess your performance in comparison to rivals, compare your KPIs to industry benchmarks. This aids in determining optimal practices and reasonable goal-setting.

Iterative Improvements: Apply modifications and monitor their effects by using the knowledge obtained from KPIs. Keep improving your tactics in light of what functions the greatest.

5. Engage Your Team in Employee Engagement: Involve your staff in the KPI process by encouraging feedback and sharing outcomes. This encourages a culture of responsibility and ongoing development.

Performance Incentives: Set performance goals for your staff members using KPIs, then provide rewards when they meet them. This encourages the finest performance possible from your team.

6. Customer Focus: Get input from customers on a regular basis and utilize it to improve your offerings. Strong client retention and satisfaction

rates are important factors in revenue development.

Tailored Care Schemes: Utilize KPI data to customize care plans to meet the requirements of each unique client. Referrals and customer satisfaction may both increase with personalized treatment.

7. Financial Management: Cost Control: Track financial KPIs to reduce expenses and boost productivity. Monitoring the typical length of a visit, for instance, can aid in scheduling caregivers more effectively.

Revenue Growth: Pay attention to KPIs like revenue per customer and client acquisition that affect revenue. Create plans to improve these KPIs, including focused advertising efforts.

Creating and applying key performance indicators (KPIs) is a great way to manage and expand your home care company. You may develop a data driven approach to business management by comprehending KPIs, finding critical indicators unique to your sector, and leveraging these analytics to generate sales and profit. This methodology not only facilitates performance monitoring but also empowers you to make well-informed decisions, efficiently manage resources, and accomplish your strategic objectives.

KPIs offer a precise, measurable method for assessing accomplishment and pinpointing areas in need of development. They assist you in maintaining focus on the important things and making sure your actions support your company's goals. You may boost customer happiness, expand sustainably and profitably, and increase the quality of care you offer by accepting KPIs and incorporating them into your management procedures.

Keep in mind that KPIs are dynamic as you put these tactics into practice. Review and modify your KPIs often to account for shifts in your company's objectives, performance, and business climate. Maintaining a competitive advantage and providing outstanding customer care need constant development. You may successfully navigate your home care business and build a robust, thriving company by implementing the appropriate KPIs.

Chapter 4

Enhancing Group Organization

For your home care business to be sustainable and operate as efficiently as possible, it is imperative that you optimize your team structure. A well-organized team works together fluidly, providing excellent treatment at a reasonable price. In order to develop a streamlined, efficient organization, this chapter will walk you through evaluating your current team, clearly defining roles and tasks, and cutting administrative costs.

Evaluating Your Present Group

It's critical to perform an extensive evaluation of your current team prior to implementing any modifications to the structure of your team. Optimizing your team will be based on a strong understanding of its dynamics, strengths, and shortcomings. Here's how to evaluate your present staff in an efficient manner:

1. Assessment of Performance:

Personal Evaluations: Make sure every team member has their performance reviewed. Take into account their abilities, contributions to the squad, and capabilities. Utilize unbiased standards and input from colleagues and customers to guarantee a thorough assessment.

Team Performance: Assess your team's general performance. Determine the team's strengths and weaknesses, as well as any gaps or inefficiencies. Examine important indicators including operational effectiveness, client satisfaction, and adherence to care plans.

2. Skill Mapping: Skill Inventory Make a skills inventory that lists all of the team members' competencies. Determine the essential abilities needed for your operations and assess how well your team currently possesses them. This aids in determining areas in need of improvement and skill shortages.

Requirements for Training: Assess the team's training requirements based on the skills inventory. Putting money into training and development can help close skill gaps and improve your team's overall performance.

3. Role Clarity and Analysis: Evaluate how well defined the roles and responsibilities are in your team. Make sure that every team member is aware of their responsibilities and how they fit into the larger goals of the company.

Recurrence and Redundancy Determine whether any responsibilities are redundant or overlap. While duplicate jobs may point to areas for simplifying, overlapping tasks can cause confusion and inefficiency.

Team Dynamics

Cooperation and Communication: Assess the team's teamwork and communication. Working as a cohesive team is essential to providing high-quality treatment. In order to promote a more cohesive work atmosphere, identify and address any communication barriers that may exist.

Group Spirit: Evaluate your team members' work satisfaction and morale. A crew that is engaged and driven is more likely to work effectively and remain loyal to the company.

You can learn a lot about your present team's strengths and places for development by doing a thorough assessment. The foundation for streamlining your team structure is this examination.

Positions and Accountabilities

To build a successful and efficient team, roles and duties must be clearly defined. There is less uncertainty and more productivity when everyone knows their part and how it fits into the bigger plan. Here's how to assign duties and obligations in an efficient manner:

1. Definition of Role:

Job descriptions: Create precise and comprehensive job descriptions for every position on your team. Provide a list of the main duties, necessary qualifications, and performance standards. Both new and existing team members can refer to job descriptions as a point of reference.

Role Structure: Clearly define a hierarchy inside your team. Establish the reporting structure and make sure that everyone is aware of their responsibilities as well as who to ask for advice or support.

2. Task Distribution: Task Evaluation: Assign the duties necessary to run your home care

company to the relevant jobs after breaking them down. Make sure the team or individual most qualified to do each work is given that assignment.

Equilibrium task: Ascertain that each team member has an equal share of the task. Underusing certain people might result in inefficiency, while overburdening others can cause burnout.

3. Accountability Assignment: Accountability: Give each task and obligation a distinct accountability. This indicates that particular people are in charge of making sure each task is finished and at a high standard.

Empowerment: Provide your team members the freedom to decide within their purview in order to empower them. This encourages accountability and a sense of ownership.

4. Versatility through Cross-Training: Promote cross-training to increase your team's adaptability. Team members can acquire new jobs through cross-training, which increases the

team's adaptability and ability to cover for absences or spikes in demand.

Career Development: Take advantage of cross-training to advance your career. It gives team members fresh knowledge and expertise, which can improve retention and job satisfaction.

A structured and effective team atmosphere is produced by clearly defined roles and duties, which let everyone know what is expected of them and how their work affects the company's overall success.

Cutting Down on Administrative Costs

Your home care business's profitability can be greatly impacted by administrative costs. You can save money on administrative expenditures without sacrificing the standard of treatment by streamlining your team structure and putting cost-cutting strategies into place. The following are some methods to cut back on administrative costs:

1. Streamlining the Process: Workflow Analysis Examine your administrative processes to find areas of inefficiency and obstruction. Simplify procedures by removing pointless stages and automating jobs that need to be done repeatedly.

SOPs, or standard operating procedures, are: Create and put into effect SOPs for standard administrative duties. SOPs guarantee efficiency and consistency, which cuts down on the time and effort needed to finish these jobs.

2. Technology Integration: Automation Tools: Make software and tool investments that can automate processes like payroll, invoicing, and scheduling. Automation lowers errors, cuts down on human labor, and frees up time for higher-value tasks.

Health Information Technology (EHR): To manage client data and care plans, implement an EHR system. EHRs decrease paperwork, increase communication, and improve data accuracy.

3. Outsourcing: NonCore Activities: Take into account contracting out non-core administrative work including IT support, HR, and accounting. For certain tasks, outsourcing can be more affordable than employing full-time personnel.

Specialized Services: For activities requiring specialized knowledge, such as legal or regulatory issues, use specialized services. This guarantees excellent service without requiring internal experts.

4. Resource Allocation: Budget Review: Examine your administrative budget on a regular basis to find areas where costs might be cut. Seek to renegotiate agreements, combine services, or come up with more affordable options.

Benefit-Cost Analysis: To make sure you are receiving the best value for your money, do cost-benefit analysis for large expenses. This facilitates the process of deciding how best to distribute resources.

5. Employee Productivity: Education and Training.

To increase the effectiveness and productivity of your administrative team, make training and development investments. Employees with proper training can finish tasks more rapidly and precisely.

Metrics of Performance: To keep an eye on the productivity of your administrative staff, use performance metrics. Determine the areas in which performance has to be enhanced and put plans in place to deal with these problems.

6. Conservation of Energy and Resources: Ecological Methods: Reduce utility bills by putting green practices into effect. Saving a lot

of money can be achieved by taking little steps like shutting off lights when not in use, purchasing energy-efficient appliances, and using less paper.

Resource Management: Keep an eye on and regulate inventory to efficiently manage resources. Make sure that supplies are not overstocked and that resources are utilized effectively.

You may lower administrative costs and strengthen the financial stability of your home care company by putting these techniques into practice. Improving the structure of your team not only increases productivity but also makes your company more profitable and long-lasting.

Effectively managing your staff structure is essential to operating a profitable home care service. You may establish an organization that is streamlined and effective by evaluating your current workforce, clearly defining roles and responsibilities, and cutting back on administrative costs. These tactics guarantee that your staff works efficiently, providing excellent service at a reasonable cost.

A cohesive team builds morale, encourages collaboration, and increases output. Having clearly defined duties and responsibilities helps to keep everyone informed and ensures that they all know their part in making the business successful. Lowering administrative costs allows you to devote more funds to customer service and business expansion.

As you put these techniques into practice, keep in mind that optimization is a continuous process. Review and modify your team structure frequently to accommodate evolving requirements and situations. Maintaining a competitive edge and providing outstanding client care require constant improvement. A well-tuned staff can help your home care company grow and reach its greatest potential.

Chapter 5

Putting Systems and Procedures in Place

Successful home care businesses are built on efficient systems and procedures. They guarantee quality, efficiency, and consistency in the provision of services. The significance of putting Standard Operating Procedures (SOPs) into practice, making use of automation tools, and encouraging a continuous improvement culture will all be covered in this chapter. You may increase productivity, lower mistakes, and improve your company's overall performance by combining these components.

SOPs, or standard operating procedures

Standard Operating Procedures (SOPs) are comprehensive, documented guidelines created to ensure consistency in the execution of particular tasks. SOPs are crucial for upholding high care standards and making sure that everyone on the team is on the same page in the setting of a home care company. Here's how to create and use SOPs that work:

1. Determine Crucial Processes:

Principal Tasks: Determine what the main functions of your home care company are first. These could involve scheduling, billing, developing a care plan for a client, and adhering to legal and regulatory regulations.

Important Assignments: Determine which essential actions within each core activity require standardization. Critical duties in client intake, for instance, may include the initial assessment, paperwork, and family communication.

2. Provide Detailed Instructions: Step-by-Step Guide: Make thorough, step-by-step instructions for every important task. Make sure the directions are straightforward to understand and follow. To ensure that all team members can understand the SOPs, use plain language and stay away from jargon.

When appropriate, incorporate visual tools like flowcharts, diagrams, and checklists. These can serve as quick references and aid in the clarification of difficult procedures.

3. Engage the Group:

Working Together: Engage your group in the creation of SOPs. To make sure that the procedures are thorough and useful, get feedback from the employees who carry out the jobs on a regular basis. Additionally, this cooperation promotes buy-in and a sense of ownership.

Review and Feedback: After the SOPs are written, go over them with your team and get their input. Adapt as needed in light of their knowledge and experiences.

4. Execute and Educate: Instructional Plans: Put training programs into place to guarantee that everyone in the team is conversant with the SOPs. To strengthen comprehension and adherence, conduct practice sessions and practical training.

Constant Monitoring: Keep an eye on how SOPs are being implemented to make sure compliance. Conducted routine audits and inspections to ensure that protocols are being appropriately followed.

5. Frequent Updates: Evaluate and Edit: Review and update SOPs frequently to account for advancements in technology, best practices, and legislation. To keep the processes relevant and efficient, keep them up to date.

Loop of Feedback: Create a feedback loop to ensure ongoing development. Invite team members to contribute updates and enhancements to the SOPs based on their practical knowledge.

You can guarantee consistency and quality in your home care services by creating and adopting SOPs. SOPs give your team a defined structure, which lowers unpredictability and increases dependability.

Automation Instruments

Your home care business's efficacy and efficiency can be greatly increased using automation systems. Your staff can focus on delivering high-quality care by freeing up crucial time by automating repetitive and time-consuming tasks. Here's how to use automation technologies to your advantage:

1. Determine Potential Automation Opportunities:
    Typical Tasks: Determine whether regular tasks—such as scheduling, invoicing, payroll,

and customer communications—can be automated. With the correct tools, these repetitive data input jobs can be made more efficient.

High-volume operations: Concentrate on high-volume operations where automation can yield the most benefits. Automated scheduling, for instance, can make it easier to efficiently handle several customer appointments.

2. Select the Appropriate Equipment:

Program Solutions: Look into and select software programs made especially for home care companies. Seek for solutions that include functions like scheduling, billing, electronic health records (EHR), and compliance management.

Capabilities for Integration: Make sure the automation tools you choose are compatible with the systems you already have in place. Data flow is improved and manual data entry is less necessary when there is seamless connection.

3. Automate: Using a Phased Approach: Use automation techniques gradually to reduce interruptions. Gradually move on to other areas, starting with one or two procedures. This step-by-step strategy gives your team flexibility and time to resolve any arising problems.

Instruction and Assistance: Give your staff thorough instruction on how to use the automation tools. Make sure they are aware of the features and advantages of the instruments. Provide continuing assistance to resolve any queries or difficulties.

4. Track and Enhance:

Performance Monitoring: Keep an eye on the automation tools' functioning at all times. To assess their efficacy, monitor data like time savings, mistake rates, and user happiness.

Optimization: Examine and improve the automated procedures on a regular basis. Seek out chances to improve functionality and efficiency. Keep up with upgrades and new features from the companies who provide your software.

5. Data Security: Safeguard Client Information: Make sure the automated solutions you employ go by best practices and data security laws. Use strong security measures to safeguard confidential client data, such as access controls and encryption.

Automation solutions can revolutionize your home care company by increasing efficiency, decreasing errors, and optimizing workflows. By using automation, you can more efficiently manage your resources and deliver better service.

Constant Enhancement

A methodical strategy to improve services, results, and processes is called continuous improvement. Establishing a culture of continuous improvement in your home care business guarantees that you are constantly working to provide your clients with the best care possible. Here's how you put a continuous improvement strategy into practice:

1. Create an Improvement Culture:

Leadership Commitment: Show that the leadership group is firmly committed to ongoing development. Establish the tone by putting quality first and promoting creativity.

Employee Engagement: Involve your group in the process of ongoing development. Invite them to point out areas that need work and offer solutions. Establish a space where ideas are respected and taken seriously.

2. Establish Improvement Objectives:

Particular Goals: Establish quantifiable, precise improvement objectives based on your strategic priorities. These objectives may have to do with financial performance, care quality, operational effectiveness, or client satisfaction.

Metrics of Performance: Track your improvement goals' progress with KPIs. Review these metrics on a regular basis to evaluate performance and pinpoint areas that still need work.

3. Put Improvement Initiatives into Practice:

Process Diagramming: To locate inefficiencies and bottlenecks in your operations, apply process mapping approaches. Create focused efforts to deal with these problems and improve workflows.

Pilot Initiatives: Pilot projects are a good way to test new concepts and upgrades. Commence modest, assess the outcome, and expand effective projects throughout the entire company.

4. Evaluation and Feedback: Staff and Client Input: Get input from employees and clients on a regular basis to find areas for development. To obtain information, do focus groups, one-on-one interviews, and surveys.

Evaluations of Performance: Review performance on a regular basis to assess the results of improvement projects. Examine information and comments to find out what went well and what needs to be changed.

5. Honor accomplishments: Acknowledgment

Honor and commemorate your team's accomplishments. Reward their efforts and acknowledge the contributions they have made to the process of continual improvement.

Exchange Knowledge: Talk to the team as a whole about the lessons and best practices that you have learned from successful improvement projects. This promotes continuous innovation and a culture of learning.

6. Ongoing Education: Instruction and Training: Make an investment in your team's ongoing education and growth. By means of conferences, workshops, and training programs, offer chances for professional development.

Remain Up to Date: Keep up with changes to regulations, industry trends, and best practices. Modify your procedures and tactics to remain on top of the game.

Using a continuous improvement strategy will help you keep your home care company innovative, adaptable, and dedicated to quality. Long-term success is supported by continuous improvement, which also fosters innovation and increases customer happiness.

Establishing efficient procedures and systems is essential to the success of your home care company. The three main components that can completely change your operations are automation tools, Standard Operating Procedures (SOPs), and a dedication to ongoing improvement. Automation technologies increase productivity and lower error rates, SOPs offer a defined foundation for consistency and quality, and continual development promotes an innovative and high-achieving culture.

You may build an organization that is streamlined, effective, and high-performing by incorporating these components into your enterprise. These tactics not only raise the standard of care you deliver, but they also raise customer happiness and long-term viability of your company. Keep in mind that optimizing your systems and processes is a continuous process as you put them into place. Maintain a competitive edge in a dynamic industry by periodically assessing, improving, and refining your processes.

Your home care business may reach its maximum potential and provide outstanding care for your clients while upholding operational excellence and financial stability if it is built upon a solid foundation of efficient systems and procedures. If you use these tactics, your company will prosper and expand while improving the lives of the people you assist.

Chapter 6

Growing Your Company

Maintaining care quality, controlling growth, and growing your home care business are all part of scaling. This chapter will offer tactics and advice on how to extend your company successfully into new markets, handle the difficulties that come with expansion, and make sure that the highest standards of care are upheld all along the way.

Taking Up New Sites

Taking your home care business to new places is a big move that needs to be carefully planned and carried out. The following are the essential factors and actions for a prosperous expansion:

1. Market research: analysis of demand Find out which areas have a high need for home care services by conducting in-depth market research. Seek out regions with aging populations, unmet healthcare needs, and a dearth of in-home caregivers.

Competitive Landscape: Examine the target area's competitive environment. Recognize the advantages and disadvantages of current suppliers and pinpoint any holes in the market that your company can close.

The regulatory landscape Learn about the rules and regulations governing the new place. Make sure your company abides by all applicable local, state, and federal laws as well as industry standards.

2. Budgeting:

Setting a budget: Create a thorough budget for the growth. Take into account expenses like office space rental, employee hire, marketing, and equipment purchase. Make sure you have enough money to sustain both the initial setup and continuing business.

Funding: Look into ways to get money to help with your growth. This could entail looking for financing, luring investors, or reinvested earnings. Make sure the aims of your firm are in line with your financial plan and that it is sustainable.

3. Choosing a Location:

Selecting a Site: Pick a prime area for your new workplace. Take into account elements like staff availability, client proximity, and accessibility. A wise choice of location can increase your exposure and draw in more business.

Facility Setup: Assemble the tools and infrastructure your office needs. Make sure the space is hospitable and furnished to meet your operational and administrative requirements.

4. Staffing: Recruitment: Assemble a group of competent experts to oversee the new site. This covers managers, caretakers, and administrative personnel. Seek out people who possess the requisite training and expertise and who share your dedication to providing high-quality care.

Training: Give your new team members thorough training. Make sure they are aware of the policies, procedures, and standards of your company. Sustaining high-quality care requires ongoing training and growth.

5. Promotion and Outreach: Local Marketing: Create a focused marketing plan to advertise your offerings in the new area. To increase awareness and draw patients, make use of neighborhood gatherings, local advertising, and alliances with medical facilities.

Online visibility: Use social media, search engine optimization (SEO), and a locally tailored website to improve your online visibility. Make it simple for prospective customers to locate you and get in touch with you.

Strategic planning and execution are necessary when expanding to new areas. You can prepare the ground for profitable expansion by carrying out in-depth research, making sound financial plans, choosing the ideal site, hiring the right people, and using efficient marketing.

Controlling Expansion

To ensure long-term success as your home care business expands, you must effectively handle the difficulties that come with it. The following tactics can be used to manage growth effectively:

1. Scalable Systems: Technology: Make an investment in expandable technology solutions to support the expansion of your company. EHR systems, scheduling programs, and communication devices fall under this category. As you grow, scalable systems support you in keeping consistency and efficiency.

Standardized procedures Create standardized procedures that are replicable in several locales. To guarantee uniformity in service delivery, SOPs, training courses, and quality assurance procedures should all be followed consistently.

2. Management and Leadership:

Strong Leadership: Assign capable managers to oversee your new sites. Good leadership is essential to upholding standards and ensuring each branch's success.

Combined Supervision: Establish centralized oversight to keep an eye on every location's performance. Make use of key performance indicators (KPIs) and frequent reporting to make sure every branch is fulfilling its objectives and upholding standards of quality.

3. Interaction:

Encourage efficient internal communication to maintain everyone on the team informed and involved. Shared best practices and alignment can be maintained with the aid of collaboration tools, newsletters, and regular meetings.

Customer Interaction: Keep lines of communication open and constant with customers and their families. Regardless of where they are getting treatment, make sure they feel included and supported.

4. Adaptability and Flexibility: 4. Adapt to Local Requirements: Be adaptable and responsive to the distinct requirements and inclinations of customers in various settings. To satisfy regional needs, allow for modification while upholding general norms.

Promoting a culture of continual improvement is important. To find opportunities for improvement and innovation, solicit input from employees and clients.

5. Administration of Finances:

Cost Control: As you expand, manage spending by putting cost control measures in place. Review financial performance on a regular basis and look for areas where you can cut costs without sacrificing quality.

Sources of Income: Investigate different revenue sources to bolster expansion. This can entail branching out into new markets, developing alliances with other healthcare providers, or providing specialized services.

Scalable systems, capable financial management, flexible scheduling, strong leadership, and efficient communication are all necessary for managing expansion. These tactics make it possible for your company to grow sustainably and uphold high standards of care.

Sustaining Care Quality

It's critical to maintain care quality as your home care business grows. Making sure every customer receives reliable, superior service is crucial to your success and reputation. Here are some tips for preserving care quality while expanding:

1. Programs for Quality Assurance:

Protocols & Standards: Establish and implement strict guidelines and procedures for the provision of care. Make sure that these guidelines are followed in every place.

Continual Evaluations: To evaluate standard compliance and pinpoint areas for improvement, conduct routine audits. To keep impartiality, employ both external and internal reviews.

2. Education and Training:

Continuous Instruction: Give your team members continual opportunity for training and development. Inform them on the most recent developments in home care, legal needs, and best practices.

Skill Development: Put your attention toward developing your team's talents. Both hard and soft skills—like empathy and communication—are included in this.

3. Customer Input:

Mechanisms of Feedback: Establish reliable methods for collecting client and family feedback. Utilize feedback forms, interviews, and surveys to learn about their experiences and pinpoint areas that need work.

Adaptive Measures: Respond to comments immediately to resolve any problems or concerns. Being receptive to customer input demonstrates your dedication to providing high-quality care.

4. Coordinating Care: Integrated Health Plans: Create integrated care plans that allow services to be coordinated between several sites. Make

sure that every client has a customized care plan that is updated frequently in accordance with their needs.

Case Management: Use efficient case management to supervise and plan the provision of care. Clients can receive thorough and consistent care with the assistance of case managers.

5. Electronic Health Record (EHR) Systems: Make use of electronic health records (EHR) to keep client data current and correct. EHR systems help with care coordination and enhance caregiver communication.

Tools for Monitoring: To monitor the delivery of care and its results, use monitoring instruments. These instruments can be used to measure performance, spot trends, and make sure care requirements are being fulfilled.

6. Employee Well-Being: Assistance and Welfare: Encourage your employees' well-being

to keep their spirits up and prevent burnout. It is more probable that contented employees will provide high-quality care.

Acknowledgment: Give your carers credit for their hard work. Giving them credit for their effort and commitment can inspire them to keep up the good work.

It takes initiative to maintain care quality while expanding. You can guarantee that your company provides continuous, high-quality care as it expands by putting quality assurance processes into place, funding training, getting and acting upon feedback, organizing care, utilizing technology, and offering assistance to your employees.

Growing your home care company is a difficult but worthwhile undertaking. You can build a strong, long-lasting company that serves more clients by branching out to new areas, controlling growth skillfully, and upholding the standard of care. Successful expansion requires careful planning, capable leadership, and a dedication to quality.

As you expand, never forget how important it is to uphold the fundamental principles and standards that characterized your early success. You can achieve long-term success and positively touch the lives of those you serve by adhering to your commitment to providing high-quality care, motivating and assisting your team, and consistently refining your operations.

Accept the chances that come with developing your company. With thoughtful planning and execution, your home care service can prosper and flourish, offering first-rate care to a clientele that is steadily increasing.

Chapter 7

Juggling Personal and Professional Life

Finding a balance between your personal and professional lives is essential because managing a home care business can be taxing and time-consuming. You need to keep this balance if you want to be healthy, productive, and successful in the long run. In order to help you attain a better work-life balance, this chapter will cover techniques for setting limits, taking care of yourself, and making long-term plans.

Defining Limits

It's critical to create distinct boundaries between work and personal life in order to avoid burnout and preserve general welfare. The following are crucial methods for creating appropriate boundaries:

1. Specify Work Schedules:
    Establish a Timetable: Set up and adhere to particular work hours. Establish clear boundaries for your workday so that it doesn't overlap with your personal time.

Establish Boundaries: Let your team and clients know what hours you work. Inform them of your availability and lack of it. This lessens disruptions during personal time and helps manage expectations.

2. Establish a Specific Work Area:
Home Office: Establish a discrete workspace apart from your living spaces if you are a remote worker. This physical division aids in drawing a

conceptual line dividing personal and professional lives.

Reduce Distractions: Make sure your work area is clear of distractions and helps you be productive. This enables you to concentrate throughout working hours and switch off at the end of the workday.

3. Prioritize Tasks: Utilize task management applications to arrange and prioritize your workload. During working hours, concentrate on high-priority projects and refrain from allowing less crucial duties to invade your leisure time.

As much as feasible, assign responsibilities to your staff. Put your trust in your employees to take care of tasks so you can concentrate on important company and personal matters.

4. Restrict Technology Use: Email Management: Assign designated hours for checking and replying to emails instead of keeping an eye on

them all day. This lessens the incentive to work past the assigned time.

Disable Notifications: When not in use, disable any unnecessary alerts. By doing this, you may detach from work and keep your personal time separate.

5. Establish Limits:

Uniform Implementation: To create a routine, firmly enforce your boundaries. Even when sustaining a healthy work-life balance is difficult, remain steadfast in your commitment to doing so.

Boundary Arrangements: Make boundary agreements with your family, coworkers, and other associates. This agreement between you and others makes sure that everyone appreciates and encourages your attempts to maintain a work-life balance.

Self-Management Techniques

Sustaining one's physical, emotional, and mental health requires self-care. Making self-care a priority helps you be your best self—personally and professionally. Here are a few successful self-care techniques:

1. Physical Well-Being: Frequent Exercise Make regular exercise a part of your schedule. Engaging in physical activity lowers stress, increases vitality, and enhances general health. Look for things to do that you enjoy, like swimming, yoga, or walking.

Healthy Eating: Keep a nutrient-rich, well-balanced diet. Eating well promotes both physical and mental well-being, which improves your capacity to manage stress and work efficiently.

2. Mental Health: Practicing Mindfulness Engages in mindfulness exercises like journaling, deep breathing, and meditation.

These techniques support mental clarity, improve focus, and lessen stress.

Mental Breaks: Throughout the day, take regular pauses to relax and refuel. Taking quick breaks can help you stay focused and avoid burnout.

3. Emotional Welfare: Social Networks: Develop your connections with friends, family, and coworkers. In addition to giving one a sense of community and belonging, social support is essential for mental wellbeing.

Emotional Expression: Give yourself permission to feel and act on your feelings. Take part in things that make you happy and fulfilled, such creative endeavors, hobbies, or time spent in nature.

4. Relaxation and Rest: Sufficient Sleep: Make obtaining enough sleep each night a priority. For emotional and physical healing, as well as for enhancing mood and cognitive performance, getting enough sleep is crucial.

Methods of Relaxation: Include relaxing activities in your routine, such as reading, taking a bath, or listening to music. These pursuits aid in relaxation and stress reduction.

5. Expert Assistance: Guidance and Treatment: Seek expert assistance if necessary. Therapy or counseling can offer helpful techniques and methods for overcoming obstacles, enhancing mental health, and controlling stress.

Mentoring: Seek the advice, perspective, and support of a mentor or coach. A mentor can support you in overcoming obstacles in work without sacrificing your personal well-being.

Extended-Term Scheduling

For your home care business to succeed in the long run and to achieve a healthy work-life balance, long-term planning is essential. The following are some methods for efficient long-term planning:

1. Clearly define your objectives: both personal and professional Establish definite professional and personal objectives. To develop a coherent future vision, match your personal goals with your corporate objectives.

SMART Objectives: To create attainable and useful goals, use the SMART criteria (Specific, Measurable, Achievable, Relevant, Timebound). You can monitor your progress and maintain focus by doing this.

2. Formulate a Concept:
Mission Statement: Create a vision statement outlining your goals for both your personal and professional life in the long run. Making decisions and setting priorities is guided by this vision.

Prospective Scheduling: As you make plans for the future, take market trends, industry developments, and possible areas for expansion into account. To maintain flexibility and resilience, be ready for everything.

3. Work-Life Integration: Equilibrium Priorities: Aim for work-life integration by striking a balance between your personal and professional obligations. Schedule personal time, hobbies, and family time in addition to work-related activities.

Adaptability Approach both your personal and professional lives with flexibility. To keep things in balance, adjust to shifting conditions and come up with novel solutions.

4. Assign and Encourage:
Group Encouragement: Delegating tasks and cultivating a climate of trust and accountability will empower your team. As a result, you have less work to do and can devote more time to personal and strategic planning.

Leadership Development: Make an investment to enhance the leadership abilities of your group. Good leaders can take care of daily tasks, freeing up your time to concentrate on long-term planning.

5. Assess and Modify:

Frequent Evaluations: Review and assess your progress toward your objectives on a regular basis. Evaluate what is going well and what needs to be changed to keep things on course.

Flexibility: Have the ability to modify your plans as necessary. It takes both flexibility and an open mind to navigate the ever-changing home care industry.

6. Succession Planning: Make Future Plans: Create a succession plan to guarantee your company's survival. Find and train future leaders who will be able to assume important positions.

Exit Plan: Think about your long-term plan for leaving. Having a clear plan guarantees a seamless transition, regardless of your plans to sell the company, transfer ownership to a family member, or take on a new role.

Striking a balance between work and personal life is a continuous process that calls for deliberate effort and thoughtful preparation. Achieving a healthier and more satisfying work-life balance can be accomplished through establishing clear boundaries, placing self-care first, and making long-term plans.

By establishing boundaries, you can keep your personal and professional lives distinct, avoid burnout, and make sure you get enough sleep and relaxation. Making self-care a priority can help you stay in optimal physical, emotional, and mental health and perform at your best in both your personal and professional life. A long-term strategy offers a route map for accomplishing your objectives and maintaining success over time.

Finding this balance as a leader in the home care industry is crucial for the success and expansion of your company as well as for your personal well-being. Ultimately, a balanced attitude leads to better results for your clients and a more fulfilling profession for you. It also makes you more focused, productive, and innovative.

Accept these tactics and resolve to give balance top priority in your life. By doing this, you'll build a strong and long-lasting home care company that will achieve your personal and professional goals.

Chapter 8

Case Studies and Success Stories

Gaining knowledge from the experiences of other industry experts in the home care sector can help you improve your own operations by offering insightful advice and doable solutions. This chapter includes real-world case studies of prosperous home care companies, along with the lessons these companies learned along the way and how you may implement these ideas into your own venture.

Real-World Instances

Sunrise Senior Care: From Success on a Local to a Regional Level

Background: In a suburban region, Sunrise Senior Care started out as a modest, family-run home care service. They had trouble at first because of their small clientele and scarce resources. However, they grew to become a top regional provider with strategic planning and efficient administration.

Important Techniques:

Client-centered strategy: Sunrise Senior Care prioritized individualized treatment and fostering close bonds with clients and their families. Referrals and client satisfaction both rose with this strategy.

Community Involvement: They worked with nearby healthcare providers and took an active part in community events. This made them more visible and solidified their reputation as a reliable local resource.

Technology Integration: To increase care coordination and streamline operations, the company made an investment in cutting-edge care management software. As a result, they were able to expand their offerings and increase efficiency.

Result: Sunrise Senior Care's clientele and income increased dramatically as a result of their regional expansion into many sites. Their reputation for providing individualized, high-quality care distinguished them from rivals.

2. Caring Healthcare Professionals: Overcoming Functional Obstacles

Background: A number of operational issues, such as a high staff turnover rate and uneven treatment quality, beset Compassionate treatment Providers. Through focused interventions, they were able to successfully transform their firm in spite of these challenges.

Important Techniques

Staff Development: They gave their caregivers access to extensive training courses and professional development possibilities. Employee satisfaction rose and turnover decreased as a result of this investment in personnel.

Quality Assurance: Regular audits, customer feedback channels, and continuous improvement projects are all part of the company's comprehensive quality assurance program. This guaranteed that every client received attention of the same caliber.

Training in Leadership: They concentrated on fostering strong leadership inside the company, enabling managers to efficiently supervise operations and assist their workforce.

Result: Compassionate treatment Providers increased the quality of their treatment, decreased staff turnover, and increased operational efficiency. In the home care sector, they have received accolades and recognition for their dedication to quality.

3. HomeCare Solutions: Quick Growth via Franchise

Context: Initially, HomeCare Solutions was a one-location home care company with plans for quick expansion. They effectively grew their business across the country by implementing a franchising strategy.

Important Techniques:

Franchise Model: They created a thorough model of franchising that included complete operating manuals, educational materials, and systems of support for franchisees. This made sure that everything was of the same caliber everywhere.
Building a Brand: To create a distinctive and reliable brand, the company made significant investments in marketing and branding

techniques. Both clients and possible franchisees were drawn to this.

Support Network: They gave franchisees continuous support, including routine training, help with marketing, and operational direction. The success of each franchise site was aided by this support system.

Result: HomeCare Solutions expanded from a single site to a network of franchises across the country. Their unified methodology and robust brand identity allowed for fast growth without sacrificing quality standards.

Knowledge Acquired

1. Client-Centered Care: Establishing a foundation of trust and loyalty requires a focus on personalized, client-centered care. Greater satisfaction and recommendations result from recognizing and attending to each client's specific demands.

Involve clients and their families in order to get input and keep improving the quality of service.

2. Community Involvement: Being actively involved in the community improves the reputation and visibility of your company. Participate in community activities, work together with nearby healthcare providers, and cultivate connections with important stakeholders.

Become known in the community as a reliable source of information by offering educational seminars, support groups, and other added-value services.

3. Technology Integration: Investing in cutting-edge technology can boost client outcomes, optimize workflow, and enhance care coordination. To assist your staff and clients, make use of communication tools, telemedicine solutions, and care management software.

Maintain a current understanding of industry innovations and best practices by routinely evaluating and updating your IT infrastructure.

4. Staff Development: Putting money into the professional growth of your employees boosts job happiness, lowers attrition, and improves the standard of care. Offer possibilities for career progression, continuous training, and a positive work environment.

Acknowledge and honor your caregivers' efforts to promote a culture of gratitude and inspiration.

5. Quality Assurance: To guarantee uniform care standards, put in place a strong program for quality assurance. Sustaining high-quality care requires ongoing improvement projects, client feedback systems, and routine audits.

Establish precise guidelines and processes to ensure that any problems or issues are dealt with quickly and efficiently.

6. Leadership and Management: Managing and expanding a profitable home care company requires strong leadership. Within your company, cultivate and enable leaders to lead teams, manage operations, and advance strategic goals.

To create a competent and durable management team, offer opportunities for leadership growth and training.

7. Franchising and Growth: If you're thinking about growing quickly, consider franchising as a potential business model. Provide thorough training materials, support systems, and franchising guides to guarantee quality and uniformity at every site.

Create a powerful brand identity and give franchisees continuous assistance to help them succeed so they can add to the overall expansion of your company.

Using Knowledge to Improve Your Company

1. Evaluate Your Current Operations: To find opportunities, threats, weaknesses, and strengths, thoroughly evaluate your current operations. Make strategic plans and decisions with this analysis in mind.

Get input from stakeholders, employees, and clients to get a complete picture of how well your company is doing and where it needs to improve.

2. Create a Strategic Plan: Create a strategic plan for your company based on the knowledge you've gathered from case studies and your evaluation. Establish deadlines for implementation, specify concrete objectives, and outline doable actions.

Make sure your strategic plan supports your long-term goals and values by coordinating it with your vision and purpose.

3. Put Best Practices into Practice: Integrate successful home care companies' best practices into your own operations. Make sure these techniques are workable and efficient by customizing them to your unique needs and situation.

Practices should be monitored and evaluated, and any necessary adjustments should be made to maximize results.

4. Promote a Culture of Continuous Improvement: Encourage your company to have a culture of continuous improvement. Review and improve your procedures, guidelines, and standards on a regular basis to improve productivity, output, and customer happiness.

Engage your staff in the process of improvement by giving them the freedom to offer suggestions and answers.

5. Make Use of Technology: Make investments in technological solutions that enhance the way

you conduct business and provide healthcare. Keep up with the latest developments and trends in the home care sector.

To monitor performance, spot trends, and come to wise judgments, use data and analytics.

6. Develop solid Relationships: Foster a solid rapport with community partners, workers, families, and clients. For long-term success, trust, cooperation, and effective communication are essential.

In order to improve your operations and services, consistently interact with your stakeholders and solicit their opinions.

7. strategy for Growth: Create a thorough strategy for expansion that takes into account elements including operational capability, financial resources, and market demand. Be ready for the advantages and disadvantages that come with growth.

Make sure your expansion strategy is in line with your mission, core principles, and dedication to providing high-quality treatment.

Gaining knowledge from other home care companies' experiences might help you succeed in your own business by offering insightful advice and successful tactics. You can improve the performance of your firm, attain sustainable growth, and uphold high standards of care by looking at real-life instances, comprehending the lessons learnt, and implementing these insights into your operations.

Growing and enhancing a home care business is a continuous process. Adopt the values of staff development, quality assurance, community involvement, client-centered care, strong leadership, and strategic planning. These components can help you reach your objectives and have a positive influence on the lives of your clients and the community when paired with a dedication to ongoing improvement.

Conclusion

Managing a Company That Doesn't Manage You

Managing a home care service is a challenging but worthwhile undertaking. We have covered a variety of tactics and ideas in this book to assist you in running your company more efficiently while taking back your personal time. The primary tactics covered will be summarized, your next steps will be outlined, and some closing views on how to keep your company journey fulfilling and sustainable will be provided in this conclusion.

Summary of Important Techniques

1. Regaining Control Over Your Time: Recognizing Time Wasters Examine your daily routine to find things that take up time but don't contribute anything. In order to concentrate on high-priority topics, eliminate or assign these activities.

Techniques for Managing Your Time: To increase efficiency and lower stress, prioritize your work, use time management applications, and create a well-organized daily schedule.

Effective Delegation: Give your team more authority by assigning duties and responsibilities. Put your trust in your personnel to take care of the operational aspects so you can focus on strategic planning and growth.

2. Establishing a Coordinated Administrative Group:

Creating Shared Objectives: Align the goals of your team with the overarching mission and vision of your company. To make sure that everyone is working toward the same goals, set explicit, quantifiable goals.

Techniques of Communication: Encourage honest and open communication among team members. Cooperation tools, feedback loops, and regular meetings can improve problem-solving and collaboration.

In charge while you're not there: Create capable executives in your company who can oversee daily operations when you're not there. Even in situations where you are not personally involved, this guarantees consistency and stability.

3. Creating Crucial KPIs:

Knowing KPIs Metrics known as key performance indicators (KPIs) assist you in gauging the efficacy and efficiency of your company's operations.

Important KPIs for Home Care Companies: To assess performance, monitor key performance indicators such customer happiness, caregiver retention, revenue growth, and operational efficiency.

Utilizing KPIs to Increase Profit and Revenue: Utilize KPI data to discover areas for development, make well-informed decisions, and put strategies into place that will increase growth and profitability.

4. Improving the Structure of the Team:

Evaluating Your Present Group: Analyze your present team's advantages and disadvantages. Create a team that is more cohesive and productive by identifying gaps and places for development.

Positions and Accountabilities: To maintain accountability and expedite processes, clearly outline each team member's tasks and responsibilities.

Cutting Down on Administrative Costs: Implement cost-cutting strategies to save administrative costs without sacrificing quality, such as automation, process optimization, and effective resource allocation.

5. System and Process Implementation: Standard Operating Procedures (SOPs): To maintain consistency in service delivery and to standardize operations, create thorough SOPs.

Automation solutions: To increase efficiency, boost accuracy, and free up time for more strategic endeavors, invest in technology and automation solutions.

Encourage a culture of continuous improvement by periodically assessing procedures, getting input, and making adjustments to increase effectiveness and caliber.

6. Growing Your Company by Adding New Locations: By carrying out market research, obtaining the required resources, and making

sure you have the operational capability to support development, you may strategically plan for expansion.

Managing Growth: Create procedures and systems that are scalable to meet rising demand. Concentrate on preserving care quality as your company expands.

Sustaining Care Quality: Keep an eye on and evaluate the standard of customer care on a constant basis. To guarantee that high standards are maintained, put in place quality assurance processes and feedback channels.

7. Juggling Professional and Personal Life:
    Establishing Limits: To avoid burnout and preserve wellbeing, clearly define the boundaries between your personal and professional lives. Establish work hours and let your team and clients know what they are.

Self-Healing Techniques: Make self-care a priority by making time for regular exercise, a balanced diet, mindfulness exercises, and enough sleep.

Extended-Term Scheduling: Create a long-term strategy that combines your personal and professional objectives. To stay on course and adjust for changing conditions, review and tweak your plan on a regular basis.

8. Success Stories and Case Studies: Actual Examples Take a lesson from other prosperous home care companies' experiences. Examine their tactics and results to acquire knowledge for your own business.

Learnings: Utilize the insights gained from these case studies in your company. Customize best practices to your unique needs and situation.

Using Knowledge to Improve Your Company: Evaluate and improve your processes on a regular basis, drawing on lessons from prosperous companies to boost output and attain long-term expansion.

Your Course of Action

As you proceed, take into account following actions to keep creating a successful home care company that supports your personal and professional goals:

1. Reflect and Evaluate: Evaluate your progress and your company methods on a regular basis. Recognize areas that need work and acknowledge accomplishments.

Get input from stakeholders, employees, and clients to get a complete picture of how well your company is performing.

2. Establish Specific Goals: Establish specific, attainable goals for your company. Make sure that these goals are consistent with your mission and long-term vision.

To create goals that can be implemented, use the SMART criteria: Specific, Measurable, Achievable, Relevant, Timebound.

3. Empower Your Team: Provide opportunities for leadership, mentorship, and training to help your team grow. A competent and driven workforce is critical to accomplishing your company's objectives.

Create a collaborative and innovative work atmosphere by being upbeat and encouraging.

4. Make Use of Technology: Keep yourself updated on developments in home care technology. Invest in equipment and processes that improve productivity, accuracy, and customer happiness.

Make educated decisions and monitor your progress toward your goals by utilizing data and analytics.

5. Maintain Balance: Put your health first by keeping a positive work-life balance. Establish limits, take care of yourself, and schedule time for things that make you happy and fulfilled.

Make plans for the future that take your personal and professional goals into account. Make sure your company aligns with your ultimate life objectives.

6. Make a Commitment to Continuous Improvement: Adopt a mindset that is focused on ongoing development. To improve quality and efficiency, evaluate and improve your procedures, guidelines, and practices on a regular basis.

Engage your staff in the process of improvement and invite them to offer suggestions and answers.

Final Words

Being a home care provider is a journey that calls for commitment, resiliency, and careful planning. Through the application of the tactics covered in this book, you may build a profitable company that doesn't control you.

Remember that creating limits, putting self-care first, and always refining your processes are the keys to striking a balance between your personal and professional lives. Utilize technology, empower your staff, and don't waver from your long-term goals.

Remember that your health and the standard of care you offer are most important as you negotiate the opportunities and difficulties presented by the home care sector. You can create a successful company that improves the lives of your customers and the community while simultaneously fostering your own success and fulfillment by keeping both things front and center.

Moving forward, you will need to keep learning and developing. Accept the trip, continue to be flexible, and aim for perfection at all times. You may accomplish your objectives and build a home care company that genuinely succeeds if you have the appropriate techniques and mindset.

www.ingramcontent.com/pod-product-compliance
Lightning Source LLC
Chambersburg PA
CBHW071520220526
45472CB00003B/1094